M

by Iain Gray

Lang**Syne**
PUBLISHING
WRITING *to* REMEMBER

Lang**Syne**

PUBLISHING

WRITING *to* REMEMBER

79 Main Street, Newtongrange,
Midlothian EH22 4NA
Tel: 0131 344 0414   Fax: 0845 075 6085
E-mail: info@lang-syne.co.uk
www.langsyneshop.co.uk

Design by Dorothy Meikle
Printed by Ricoh Print Scotland
© Lang Syne Publishers Ltd 2012

All rights reserved. No part of this publication may be reproduced, stored or introduced into a retrieval system, or transmitted in any form or by any means (electronic, mechanical, photocopying, recording or otherwise) without the prior written permission of Lang Syne Publishers Ltd.

ISBN 978-1-85217-470-5

Mason

MOTTO:
While I breathe I have hope.

CREST:
A mermaid with comb and glass.

NAME variations include:
  Machin
  Machon
  Massen
  Masson
  Massons
  Clacher *(Gaelic)*

*Echoes of a far distant past
can still be found in most names*

Chapter one:

Origins of Scottish surnames

by George Forbes

It all began with the Normans.

For it was they who introduced surnames into common usage more than a thousand years ago, initially based on the title of their estates, local villages and chateaux in France to distinguish and identify these landholdings, usually acquired at the point of a bloodstained sword.

Such grand descriptions also helped enhance the prestige of these arrogant warlords and generally glorify their lofty positions high above the humble serfs slaving away below in the pecking order who only had single names, often with Biblical connotations as in Pierre and Jacques.

The only descriptive distinctions among this peasantry concerned their occupations, like Pierre the swineherd or Jacques the ferryman.

The Normans themselves were originally Vikings (or Northmen) who raided, colonised and eventually settled down around the French coastline.

They had sailed up the Seine in their longboats in 900 AD under their ferocious leader Rollo and ruled the roost in north east France before sailing over to conquer England, bringing their relatively new tradition of having surnames with them.

It took another hundred years for the Normans to percolate northwards and surnames did not begin to appear in Scotland until the thirteenth century.

These adventurous knights brought an aura of chivalry with them and it was said no damsel of any distinction would marry a man unless he had at least two names.

The family names included that of Scotland's great hero Robert De Brus and his compatriots were warriors from families like the De Morevils, De Umphravils, De Berkelais, De Quincis, De Viponts and De Vaux.

As the knights settled the boundaries of their vast estates, they took territorial names, as in Hamilton, Moray, Crawford, Cunningham, Dunbar, Ross, Wemyss, Dundas, Galloway, Renfrew, Greenhill, Hazelwood, Sandylands and Church-hill.

Other names, though not with any obvious geographical or topographical features, nevertheless derived from ancient parishes like Douglas, Forbes, Dalyell and Guthrie.

Other surnames were coined in connection with occupations, castles or legendary deeds. Stuart originated in the word steward, a prestigious post which was an integral part of any large medieval household. The same applied to Cooks, Chamberlains, Constables and Porters.

Borders towns and forts – needed in areas like the Debateable Lands which were constantly fought over by feuding local families – had their own distinctive names; and it was often from them that the resident groups took their communal titles, as in the Grahams of Annandale, the Elliots and Armstrongs of the East Marches, the Scotts and Kerrs of Teviotdale and Eskdale.

Even physical attributes crept into surnames, as in Small, Little and More (the latter being 'beg' in Gaelic), Long or Lang, Stark, Stout, Strong or Strang and even Jolly.

Mieklejohns would have had the strength of several men, while Littlejohn was named after the legendary sidekick of Robin Hood.

Colours got into the act with Black, White, Grey, Brown and Green (Red developed into Reid,

Ruddy or Ruddiman). Blue was rare and nobody ever wanted to be associated with yellow.

Pompous worthies took the name Wiseman, Goodman and Goodall.

Words intimating the sons of leading figures were soon affiliated into the language as in Johnson, Adamson, Richardson and Thomson, while the Norman equivalent of Fitz (from the French-Latin 'filius' meaning 'son') cropped up in Fitzmaurice and Fitzgerald.

The prefix 'Mac' was 'son of' in Gaelic and clans often originated with occupations – as in MacNab being sons of the Abbot, MacPherson and MacVicar being sons of the minister and MacIntosh being sons of the chief.

The church's influence could be found in the names Kirk, Clerk, Clarke, Bishop, Friar and Monk. Proctor came from a church official, Singer and Sangster from choristers, Gilchrist and Gillies from Christ's servant, Mitchell, Gilmory and Gilmour from servants of St Michael and Mary, Malcolm from a servant of Columba and Gillespie from a bishop's servant.

The rudimentary medical profession was represented by Barber (a trade which also once included dentistry and surgery) as well as Leech or Leitch.

Businessmen produced Merchants, Mercers, Monypennies, Chapmans, Sellers and Scales, while down at the old village watermill the names that cropped up included Miller, Walker and Fuller.

Other self explanatory trades included Coopers, Brands, Barkers, Tanners, Skinners, Brewsters and Brewers, Tailors, Saddlers, Wrights, Cartwrights, Smiths, Harpers, Joiners, Sawyers, Masons and Plumbers.

Even the scenery was utilised as in Craig, Moor, Hill, Glen, Wood and Forrest.

Rank, whether high or low, took its place with Laird, Barron, Knight, Tennant, Farmer, Husband, Granger, Grieve, Shepherd, Shearer and Fletcher.

The hunt and the chase supplied Hunter, Falconer, Fowler, Fox, Forrester, Archer and Spearman.

The renowned medieval historian Froissart, who eulogised about the romantic deeds of chivalry (and who condemned Scotland as being a poverty stricken wasteland), once sniffily dismissed the peasantry of his native France as the jacquerie (or the jacques-without-names) but it was these same humble folk who ended up overthrowing the arrogant aristocracy.

In the olden days, only the blueblooded knights of antiquity were entitled to full, proper names, both Christian and surnames, but with the passing of time and a more egalitarian, less feudal atmosphere, more respectful and worthy titles spread throughout the populace as a whole.

Echoes of a far distant past can still be found in most names and they can be borne with pride in commemoration of past generations who fought and toiled in some capacity or other to make our nation what it now is, for good or ill.

Chapter two:

The Mason Craft

An occupational surname originally referring to someone who worked with stone, 'Mason' and its numerous spelling variants that include 'Masson' is derived from the Old French *machun* or *macon*.

First introduced to British shores in the wake of the Norman Conquest of 1066, it subsequently grew in popularity as a name because of the high number of masons, or stonemasons, required for the elaborate construction of not only magnificent churches and cathedrals but also castles and other imposing structures for royalty and others of power and substance.

The name has a Gaelic form, *Clacher*, although the mason craft was not in particularly high demand in the Highlands and Islands.

As early as 1271, a 'Richard the Mason' appears in the historical record in Aberdeen, a William Maceoun in Berwick in 1320 and Thomas Mason in Coupar Angus in 1490.

It was not until the mid to late seventeenth century that the name began to appear in Ireland –

largely through the harsh policy of 'Plantation', that involved the settling of loyal subjects on lands previously held by those deemed to be 'rebellious' native Irish.

The history of the mason craft in Scotland and therefore that of the Mason name is particularly intriguing.

Masons employed on building projects were organised into lodges, the name originally given to where they lived, or found lodgings.

In common with other skilled trades, they had their own system of secret passwords, handshakes and other forms of recognition to guard against outsiders or unskilled masons encroaching on their territory.

Known as Craft Masonry, this later moved away from being the exclusive preserve of working, or operative, stonemasons, to make way for non-operative, or speculative, Freemasons.

It was from Scottish Freemasonic practice that the three basic 'Craft' degrees of Entered Apprentice, Fellow Craft and Master Mason became established – although originally in Scotland, Fellow Craft and Master Mason formed part of the one degree, or grade.

It is through their link to the craft of masonry

and, in turn, Freemasonry, that bearers of the Mason name have a curious link to one of Scotland's most distinguished clans – that of Clan Sinclair.

So close is this link that, along with other families who include those of Caird, Clouston, Clyne, Laird, Lyall, Purdie, Linklater and Snoddy, they are recognised as a sept, or sub-branch, of the clan.

As a sept of the Sinclairs, these families shared in not only the clan's glorious fortunes, but also its tragic misfortunes.

With their motto of *Commit thy work to God* and crest of a cock, their Gaelic name is *Clann-na-Cearda*, Children of the Craft, or Craftsmen.

Their roots lie in distant Norway, from where they embarked in their longships to raid, ravage and pillage before settling in what became known as Norse-man's-land, better known as Normandy, in France. Later they settled on British shores in the wake of the Norman Conquest.

Becoming established in Scotland with territory in Midlothian, Caithness and Orkney, the Sinclairs and their kinsfolk such as the Masons not only played a prominent role in Scotland's turbulent history, but are reputed to be the custodians of a secret tradition.

This is a tradition said to relate to the bloodline of Jesus and one which came to the attention of a much wider international audience in 2003with the publication of the Dan Brown novel *The Da Vinci Code* and the release of the film of the name three years later, starring Tom Hanks and Audrey Tauto.

Standing on the edge of the scenic Esk Valley near the village of Roslin, in Midlothian, and attracting thousands of visitors every year – particularly after the release of *The Da Vinci Code* film in which it features – is the mysterious Rosslyn Chapel.

This famous edifice was built in 1446 by William Sinclair, who was created Lord Sinclair in 1449.

Founded as a collegiate church and consecrated to St Matthew it is thought to encode in stone a mystery that links a band of warrior monks who were known as the Knights Templar, the origins of Scottish Freemasonry and a secret relating to the Holy Grail.

It had been intended that the chapel be built in the form of a cross, with a tower in the centre but it was never completed; only the east transept and the choir were built.

Built in a style described as 'florid Gothic', it

is famous for its Apprentice's Pillar, which stands in the south east corner.

Decorated with four wreaths of flowers, spiralling from base to crown, it is the subject of a curious legend that the Master Mason, jealous of the skill of a young apprentice who sculpted the pillar, killed him with a blow to the forehead.

With strange echoes of Freemasonic legend, three stone heads at the west of the chapel commemorate this slaying.

One is thought to be the apprentice's mother, and is known as The Widowed Mother, while one depicts the apprentice with a gash above his right eye, and the other depicts the Master Mason.

This is taken as evidence that the masons who built the chapel were privy to esoteric knowledge that had been transmitted to them through those Knights Templar who had sought refuge in Scotland after being outlawed by Papal Bull in 1307.

The Templars, who had been formed in 1118 to guard the pilgrim routes to the Holy Land, are thought to have excavated the ruins of Solomon's Temple in Jerusalem, and unearthed an awesome secret relating to Christianity.

Some claim the secret may have been in the

form of ancient parchments – or even the famed Holy Grail of the Last Supper itself.

Another controversial theory is that the grail may not be an actual vessel, or cup, but a secret relating to the bloodline of Christ.

A persistent claim is that a body of refugee Templars fought on the side of Robert the Bruce at Bannockburn, and that their secret knowledge was later transmitted, through what became Scottish Freemasonry, to some of Scotland's noblest families, including the Sinclairs.

Sir William Sinclair, some believe, may actually have built Rosslyn Chapel as a repository for the secrets of the Templars.

Twelve Sinclair barons are known to be buried in sealed vaults beneath the chapel, laid to rest in full armour.

Who knows what else may lay gathering the dust of centuries in these sealed vaults?

There is a tradition that, in 1441, James II appointed a Sinclair of Rosslyn as Patron and Protector of Scottish Masons, and that that the office was hereditary.

In 1628 a charter was drawn up by William Schaw, Master of Works to James VI that sought to obtain from the king the right of the Sinclairs to be recognised as having jurisdiction over masons as patrons and judges.

The Charter argued that it has been recognised from age to age that the Lairds of Roslin had been patrons and protectors of the Craft and its privileges, and that this had 'died out through neglect'.

In 1736, it was a Sinclair of Rosslyn who was appointed the first Grand Master of the (Freemasonic) Grand Lodge of Scotland after having renounced his hereditary claims to the title.

On the field of battle, William Sinclair was one of the twelve Earls who fell with his king, James IV, at the disastrous Battle of Flodden in 1513.

So great was the slaughter among the Sinclairs of Caithness and their kinsfolk such as the Masons, that to this day there is a tradition they have an aversion to wearing the colour green or crossing over the Ord Hill on a Monday – because it was on a Monday, clothed in green, that they marched over the Ord Hill on their way to Flodden Field.

The Sinclairs and their kinsfolk had also fought in the cause of Scotland's freedom in 1314 at Bannockburn, while Sir William Sinclair and his brother John Sinclair were among the knights who accompanied Sir James Douglas on a mission in 1330 to bury the heart of the great warrior king Bruce in the Holy Land.

Attacked by Moors while travelling through Spain, Lord James and the two Sinclair brothers were killed, but the heart of Bruce was returned to Scotland and buried in the grounds of Melrose Abbey, in the Borders.

Robert the Bruce, King of Scots — The Victor of Bannockburn

Chapter three:

Politics and exploration

Away from the battlefield and from a history entwined with that of the Sinclairs, bearers of the Mason name have gained distinction and honours.

Considered one of the Founding Fathers of the United States, George Mason IV was the American patriot and statesman born in 1725 into a prominent family of Virginia planters.

As a delegate from Virginia to the U.S. Constitutional Convention he, along with James Madison, is also considered the Father of the Bill of Rights, enshrined in the Constitution as ten important amendments and ratified in 1791.

It is through the Bill of Rights that specific State and also individual rights are assured.

He died in 1792, while he is honoured through the George Mason Memorial in West Potomac Park, Washington D.C., Mason County, West Virginia, Mason County, Kentucky and Mason County, Illinois.

In British politics, Roy Mason is the former coal miner and Labour Party politician honoured in the

Peerage of the United Kingdom as Lord Mason of Barnsley.

Born in 1924 in Royston, South Yorkshire, he went down the mines at the age of 14 and continued working in the coal industry until first elected for the constituency of Barnsley in 1953.

Before retiring as a Member of Parliament (MP) at the 1987 General Election, he had held an impressive list of Cabinet posts that included, from 1969 to 1970, President of the Board of Trade, Secretary of State for Defence between 1974 and 1976 and, from 1976 to 1979, Secretary of State for Northern Ireland.

In Australia, Sir Anthony Mason, born in Sydney in 1925, is the former lawyer who, from 1972 to 1995, served as Chief Justice of the High Court of Australia.

From politics and law to the decidedly less contentious landscape of horticulture, one notably green-fingered bearer of the Mason name – in the equally popular form of Masson – was the Scottish botanist, plant collector and gardener Francis Masson.

Born in Aberdeen in 1741, he began work as an under-gardener at Kew Gardens, London, in the early 1760s.

Appointed only a few short years later as Kew's first official plant collector, he sailed aboard the explorer Captain James Cook's *HMS Resolution* in 1772, collecting previously unknown plant species from South Africa and North America.

Further expeditions followed to parts that included Madeira, the Canary Islands, the Azores, the Antilles and Portugal.

Only returning to Kew for brief periods to deliver his rare specimens before setting off again on further expeditions, he discovered more than 1,700 new species that include the Bird of Paradise Flower, Red Hot Poker and the Arum Lily.

He was on expedition when he died in Montreal in 1805.

Named in his honour is the genus of plants *Massonia*, while there is also a commemorative plaque to him in the Cruickshank Botanic Garden, Old Aberdeen.

Bearers of the name have also excelled in the highly competitive world of business.

Recognised as having been Canada's first French-Canadian millionaire, Joseph Masson was born in 1791 in Saint-Eustache, in what was then Lower Canada.

In partnership from 1812 with the Scottish merchant Hugh Robertson in the lucrative import and export business, by 1832 he was involved in his own right in a number of major Canadian infrastructure projects and developments.

These included founding the country's first railway, the Champlain and St Lawrence Railroad, while in 1841 he was co-founder of what has become today's thriving city of Toronto.

Also with interests in a number of banks, including the Bank of Montreal and the Bank of Canada, he died, the country's wealthiest man at the time, in 1847.

Also in North America, Charles Mason, born in 1728 in Stroud, Gloucestershire was the English surveyor and astronomer whose surname forms part of a famous description of an American geographical feature.

This is the Mason-Dixon Line, marking the division between the northern and the southern United States, and which was surveyed by Mason and Jeremiah Dixon between 1764 and 1768.

Also an assistant astronomer at the Greenwich Observatory, London, he died in 1786, while the moon crater Mason is named in his honour.

Back to the world of wars and rebellion in which bearers of the Mason name frequently found themselves, Martin Mason was the surgeon and magistrate born in Cumbria, in the north of England, in 1765.

Arriving as a surgeon in Sydney in 1798, he set up Australia's first medical practice, at Green Hills, now the Windsor area of Sydney.

But in 1808 he became embroiled in what was known as the Rum Rebellion – in which settlers rose up and deposed the unpopular William Bligh, British colonial governor of New South Wales.

Mason had supported Bligh and was summoned as a witness to a subsequent trial in London in 1810 of captured rebel leaders.

His damning evidence against the rebels proved highly unpopular among their supporters, and Mason mysteriously disappeared – presumed murdered – before he was supposed to embark from London after the trial on the vessel that was to have taken him back to Australia.

On the battlefields of the Second World War, Leonard Mason was a posthumous recipient of the Medal of Honor, America's highest military award for valour in the face of enemy action.

He had been a Private First Class (PFC) in the United States Marine Corps when, in July of 1944 during the war in the Pacific, he was killed on the island of Guam after single-handedly clearing out a Japanese machine-gun position, despite having already been seriously wounded.

One of the weapons that Mason may well have carried was one first invented nearly 80 years earlier by William Mason.

Born in 1837 in Oswego, New York, he was the engineer and inventor who, working for the Colt firearms company along with Charles Richards, in 1869 designed the rear-loading metallic cartridge revolver that developed into the famous Colt 45 – with '45' indicating the bullet calibre.

An inaugural member of the American Society of Mechanical Engineers and having patented more than 120 designs during his lifetime, not only for firearms but also for steam pumps and power looms, he died in 1913.

Chapter four:

On the world stage

Bearers of the Mason name and its equally popular form of Masson have stamped their mark at an international level through a colourful variety of pursuits.

Despite not having had any formal training as an actor, **James Mason** went on to receive a number of film honours.

Born in 1909 in Yorkshire, the son of a wealthy merchant, he gained a degree in architecture from Cambridge University, where he also became involved in a number of small theatrical productions.

A conscientious objector during the Second World War, he instead became the star of a number of British film melodramas during the war years that included the 1943 *The Man in Grey* and the 1945 *The Wicked Lady*.

International stardom came with his role in the 1945 *The Seventh Veil* and his first Hollywood film, *Caught*, came four years later.

His many awards include an Academy Award nomination for the 1982 *The Verdict*, while other film credits include the 1944 *Fanny by Gaslight*, the 1951 *The Desert Fox: The Story of Rommel*, director Alfred Hitchcock's 1959 *North by Northwest* and, in the year of his death in 1984, *The Assisi Underground*.

Married to the actress Pamela Mason, he was the father of the American actor, film producer and politician **Morgan Mason**, born in Beverley Hills, California, in 1955.

As a young boy, he appeared in films that include *The Sandpiper*, which starred Elizabeth Taylor and Richard Burton, while he also served as Special Assistant to former U.S. President Ronald Reagan.

Married to the singer Belinda Carlisle, he is the father of the film producer **James Duke Mason**, who's 1989 *Sex, Lies and Videotape* was the winner of the Palme d'Or at the Cannes Film Festival.

Married to the playwright Neil Simon since he cast her in his 1973 Broadway play *The Good Doctor*, **Marsha Mason** is the American actress and television director born in 1942 in St Louis, Missouri.

Director of the 1987 *Little Miss Perfect*, she is the recipient of four Academy Award nominations that include one for Best Actress for her role in the 1973 *Cinderella Liberty*, in which she co-starred with James Caan.

Her other nominations for Best Actress were for the 1977 *The Goodbye Girl*, based on a play by her husband, the 1979 *Chapter Two* and, in 1981, *The Gingerbread Lady*.

An artistic associate of the National Theatre of Scotland, **Forbes Masson**, born in Falkirk in 1963, is the Scottish actor and writer who in the 1980s had a successful comedy partnership with fellow Scottish actor Alan Cumming as the musical double act Victor and Barry. He performed with the Royal Shakespeare Company from 2003 to 2011, while it was with Cumming that he co-wrote the television sitcom *The High Life*.

Born in 1936 in Sheboygan, Wisconsin, but growing up on the Lower East Side of Manhattan, Yacov Moshe Maza is the American stand-up comedian and actor better known as **Jackie Mason**.

Following a family tradition, he was ordained as a rabbi of the Jewish faith at the age of 25, but abandoned this three years later in favour of a career as a comedian.

Voted in 2005 by fellow comedians and comedy critics as among the top 50 comedy acts of all time, he is also the recipient of an Emmy Award for his voice-over – of a rabbi – in an episode of *The Simpsons*.

Bearers of the Mason name have also excelled in the highly competitive world of sport.

Awarded the title of Master Gymnast by British Gymnastics, **Lisa Mason** is the former gymnast who first took up the discipline at the age of only five.

Born in 1982 in Aylesbury, Buckinghamshire, she won two gold medals at the 1998 Commonwealth Games and has held the title of British Gymnastic Champion on three occasions – the first being at the age of 14.

In the boxing ring, **Gary Mason**, born in 1962 in Jamaica, was the boxer who took the British heavyweight championship title in 1989.

In a career that lasted from 1984 to 1994, Mason, who was killed in a road accident in 2011, had an impressive 37 wins out of 38 fights.

In the creative world of the written word, **Robert Mason**, born in 1942 in Plainfield, New Jersey, is the Vietnam War veteran and author whose best-selling memoir is the 1983 *Chickenhawk*.

A former helicopter pilot to the 1st Cavalry Division (Airmobile), his other books include *Weapon* and *Solo*.

Born in 1919 near Manchester, **Richard Mason** was the British novelist whose 1957 *The*

World of Suzie Wong was adopted as a Broadway play and also as a film of the same name in 1960, starring William Holden and Nancy Kwan in the title role.

An interrogator of Japanese prisoners of war during the Second World War, he later settled in Hong Kong, while his 1950 novel *The Shadow and the Peak*, was filmed as *Passionate Summer*, starring Dirk Bogarde; he died in 1997.

Author of the 1937 novel *Fire Over England*, which uncannily foresaw the aerial blitz on London during the Second World War, **Alfred Mason** was the author and politician born in 1865 in Dulwich, London. Liberal Member of Parliament (MP) for Coventry from 1906 to1910, he is also remembered for his 1902 novel *The Four Feathers*; he died in 1948.

Not only an author, artist and filmmaker but also a naturalist and conservationist, **Bill Mason** was born in 1929 in Winnipeg, Manitoba.

Roaming widely across the wilderness areas of both his native Canada and the United States, often by canoe, he is particularly noted for his best-selling canoeing books, nature films and documentaries on wolves.

Known as the "wilderness artist", his books include *Path of the Paddle* and *Canoescapes*, while his

1962 film *Wilderness Treasure* was the winner of a Canadian Film Award.

Also the recipient of a number of honours, including an Academy Award nomination in 1968 for Best Short Film for *Paddle to the Sea*, he died in 1988.

Appointed to the prestigious post of Historiographer Royal for Scotland in 1893 and also a chairman of the Scottish History Society, **Sir David Masson** was the Scottish literary critic and historian born in 1822 in Aberdeen.

Contributor to a number of publications and also appointed professor of English literature at University College, London, in 1893, he died in 1907.

He was the father of **Sir David Orme Masson** who, pursuing a much different career from that of his father became professor of chemistry at Melbourne University after immigrating to Canada.

Born in Hampstead, London, in 1858, he founded the Society of Chemical Industry of Victoria and the Australian Chemical Institute; he died in 1937.

One of his grandsons, **David Irvine Masson**, born in Edinburgh in 1915 and who died in 2007, was the British science fiction writer whose works include *The Caltraps of Time* collection of short stories.

In the world of music, **Nick Mason**, born in

1944 in Birmingham, is the English drummer and songwriter best known as a member since its formation in 1965 of the band Pink Floyd.

Co-writer of Pink Floyd music that includes *Interstellar Overdrive*, from the 1967 album *Piper at the Gates of Dawn and Time*, he is also a motor racing enthusiast – having competed in events that include the 24 Hours of Le Mans.

Born in 1946 in Worcester, **Dave Mason** is the English singer, songwriter and guitarist known for his work with the 1960s rock band Traffic and as the writer of their hit songs *Hole in My Shoe* and *Feelin' Alright*.

A solo, orchestral and recording session trumpet player, **David Mason** was the musician born in London in 1926 and who died in 2011.

He contributed to a number of Beatles songs as a session musician – most notably the piccolo trumpet solo on the 1967 *Penny Lane*.

Known as "Prime Minister of the Blues", **Dutch Mason** was the legendary Canadian singer, pianist and guitarist born Norman Byron Mason in Lunenburg, Nova Scotia, in 1938.

Known for recordings that include his 1971 *Putting It Altogether* and the 2004 *Half Ain't Been Told*, he is an inductee of the Canadian Jazz and Blues Hall of Fame and the Order of Canada; he died in 2006.

In the vibrant world of art, **Frank Mason**, born in 1875 in Hartlepool, Co. Durham was the English artist noted for his coastal harbour and maritime paintings and as the creator of art deco travel and railway posters.

A member of the Royal Society of British Artists and the Royal Institute of Painters in Water Colours, he died in 1965.

Two particularly inventive bearers of the Mason name were the Americans **Samuel Mason** and **John Landis Mason**.

Born in New York City in 1921, Samuel Mason was the electronics engineer who developed special tactile devices powered by photocells that enable the blind to sense light.

Also before his death in 1974, he gave his name to Mason's Rule – a method used in the field of control systems theory.

A tinsmith to trade, John Landis Mason, born in Philadelphia in 1832 and who died in 1902, invented not only the metal screw-on lid for jars now known as Mason Jars, but also, in 1858, the first screw-top salt shaker.